W9-CAY-411

An Amish Portrait

SONG OF A PEOPLE

An Amish Portrait
SONG OF A PEOPLE

Text by
Merle Good

Photography by
Jerry Irwin

Good Books

Intercourse, PA 17534

Design by Dawn J. Ranck

AN AMISH PORTRAIT: SONG OF A PEOPLE
Copyright © 1993 by Good Books, Intercourse, Pennsylvania 17534
First published in 1993 (ISBN: 1-56148-095-9)
REVISED EDITION, 1997.
International Standard Book Number: 1-56148-238-2
Library of Congress Catalog Card Number: 93-30733

Printed in China

Library of Congress Cataloging-in-Publication Data

Good, Merle.
    An Amish portrait : song of a people / text by Merle Good ;
photography by Jerry Irwin
        p. cm.
    1. Amish--Pictorial works. 2. Amish--poetry. I. Irwin, Jerry.
II. Title.
E185.M45G663 1993
908'.8287--dc20   93-30733
                                                            CIP

Introduction

Belonging to a people is a precious thing. The Old Order Amish know this. They are sustained by an abiding sense of community, the spirit of historic faith, the call of discipline, and the joyful restraint of beauty.

Yet life for the Amish is not a fairy tale. They, too, are visited by disappointment, grief, and failure. But on balance, the embrace of community, the harvest after the toil, the peace from following God, and the promise in the eyes of the young people all lead to a deep sense of contentment.

A portrait of the Amish way shines with color, strength, endurance, and fulfillment.

—Merle Good

We watch the past

create the now—

And wish to plant

before we plow—

We hear "goodbye"

in each hello—

And wish to stay

when we must go—

We seek for peace

in time of war—

And watch the rich

receive the poor—

As day makes night

a fugitive—

FOR SALE
1 owner - low miles

The living dream,
the dreaming live.

An Amish Portrait

For more than 300 years, the Amish people have endeavored to live out their ideals. Today there are approximately 160,000 adults and children who follow the Old Order Amish way. These people live in dozens of communities scattered across 22 states and one Canadian province. (Ohio, Pennsylvania, and Indiana are home to three-fourths of the Amish.)

A Dynamic Faith

It is impossible to understand the Amish without grasping the centrality of their Christian faith in everything they do. Theirs is not a static culture or a dying curiosity, as some would suggest. The Amish have, in fact, more than doubled in church membership during the past twenty years.

Simplicity, humility, steadfastness, modesty, and serving others before self—these characteristics of Christ are held up as models of living for followers of the Christian way. Their living of these qualities partly explains why the Amish leave so many persons in today's world at once both charmed and nonplussed. The values of Amish society largely run counter to those of the modern world.

A Rich Family Life

Children are cherished, the elderly are respected, and the extended family is cultivated among the Amish. An Amish person lives an entire life surrounded by the embrace of that network of family and church community. The individual submits to the larger group, but hopefully does not feel suffocated or unduly submerged by this way of life.

The greatest achievement possible for an Amish child is to grow up to be a committed member of the faith community. Such a perspective sets limits, but also can lead to contentment.

Learning and/or Wisdom

The Amish do not exalt ignorance, but neither do they put learning on a pedestal, as much of modern culture does. Information is helpful; too much information, they believe, may seem unnecessary, even worldly, and potentially destructive to community life. Extolling one individual's accumulation of information and knowledge almost always leads to division, pride, and jealousy, in their view.

Wisdom should be sought after, the Amish believe. Learning is fine, within limits, but wisdom forms the soul of life. Wisdom is a gift from God, gained from humility, discipline, learning, and a grateful heart.

The Amish school prepares young people for the Amish way. Wisdom is stressed more than knowledge. The lessons teach basics of reading, writing, and math. Religion is taught at church and at home. The Amish children normally attend one-room and two-room schools, and are exempt from modern high schools.

Caring for God's Earth

Most Amish prefer farming to other vocations, even though more and more are needing to work away from home. These people believe in caring for the soil, both the bountiful fields and the colorful gardens.

The Amish are known as some of the world's best farmers. This stems partly from their carefulness in selecting land. But their sense of stewardship before God and their belief that hard work is a good thing certainly contribute to the plentiful harvests.

Machines Often Separate People

Why no cars? Why so few modern conveniences?

The Amish stubbornly resist the constant attempts of modern

machines to separate them from each other. Cars bring independence, greater distances, a dramatic sense of power—and cars tend to break up families at meals and at many other times. Microwave ovens can do the same. The test for the Amish, on a case by case basis, is rather simple—will this machine enhance community or erode it?

A Sense of Heritage

The Amish date their beginnings to the Anabaptists (later called Mennonites) in Switzerland, Germany, and The Netherlands in the early 1500s. In 1693, however, the Amish broke with the Mennonites because they felt Mennonites were becoming too lenient, careless, and casual about their faith and practice. This renewal movement was led by Jacob Amman.

Drawing Lines

How can one know where the center is if one does not know where the edge is?

Part of the success of the Amish church during the past 100 years has been its careful development of boundaries to nourish the heart of its vision. Every aspect of life has its limits defined.

This seems unnecessarily restrictive to outsiders, and to some within. But the intentional drawing of lines requires deliberate decision-making, and the vast majority of Amish young people are embracing this way of life and faith as their own.

Seasons of Life

These people accept the ebb and flow of life as natural. Dawn follows the night, as winter comes after harvest. Tears are mixed with the contentment and the joy.

The Amish people are not perfect. They are the first to say so. But the strength of their commitment in a world which shuns commitment, the appeal of their simplicity and peaceful humility in a world that screams for attention, and the joyful embrace of their community in a world bent on "everyone for one's self" articulates through quiet lives a harmony which makes many moderns wistful.

—Merle Good

To Learn More about the Amish

For more information about the Amish, write to or visit The People's Place, 3513 Old Philadelphia Pike, Intercourse, PA 17534, an Amish and Mennonite heritage center (of which Merle Good and his wife Phyllis are Executive Directors.) Or request a free list of books about the Amish.

About the Author

Merle Good has written numerous books and articles about the Amish, including the beautiful book *Who Are the Amish?* and the popular children's books *Reuben and the Fire* and *Reuben and the Blizzard* (artwork by P. Buckley Moss). In addition to The People's Place, he and his wife Phyllis oversee a series of projects in publishing and the arts. They have also authored many books, including *20 Most Asked Questions About the Amish and Mennonites,* as well as *Christmas Ideas for Families.* They live in Lancaster, PA with their two daughters.

About the Photographer

Jerry Irwin's photography has appeared in a series of books and in many national publications. He lives near Paradise, PA.